MAJOR LEAGUE BASEBALL®

BASEBALL COUNTRY

Written by the Editors of Major League Baseball

MAJOR LEAGUE BASEBALL PROPERTIES, INC.

contents

Major League Baseball: Baseball Country was developed, written and designed by the publishing department of Major League Baseball Properties, Inc.

ISBN 0-9776476-0-9

First Printing: January 2006

PHOTO CREDITS © MLB Photos: Rich Pilling (Fisk, White Sox, Brett, Puckett, Ryan, Yount, Martinez, Schmidt, Legends Field, Tempe Diablo Stadium, Hiram Bithorn Stadium); Ron Vesely (Hafner, Ichiro p. 16, Baldelli, Barmes); Louis Requena (Kaline, Aaron, Koufax, Mays); Rob Leiter (Guerrero, Gonzalez); NBLA (Ruth); Brad Mangin (Chavez); Rob Skeoch (Carter); Stephen Green (Prior, Biggio); John Grieshop (Great American Ball Park, Bay, Pujols); Michael Zagaris (Morgan); Eliot Schechter (Willis); Dan Donovan (Busch Stadium); Jon SooHoo (Gwynn); Mitchell Layton (Hernandez). **© Getty Images:** Jamie Squire (Oriole Park at Camden Yards, Citizens Bank Park, RFK Stadium); Jim McIsaac (Fenway Park, U.S. Cellular Field); Jonathan Daniel (Jacobs Field, Miller Park); Harry How/Allsport (Comerica Park); Brian Bahr (Kauffman Stadium, Coors Field); Christian Petersen (Angel Stadium, Petco Park); Lisa Blumenfeld (Metrodome, Dodger Stadium); Ezra Shaw (Yankee Stadium, Dolphins Stadium, Hall of Fame); Jed Jacobsohn (McAfee Coliseum, SBC Park); Otto Greule Jr. (Safeco Field, Ichiro p. 43); Doug Pensinger (Ripken); Nick Laham (Tropicana Field); Ronald Martinez (Ameriquest Field, Minute Maid Park); Rick Stewart (Rogers Centre, PNC Park); Todd Warshaw/Allsport (Chase Field); Scott Cunningham (Turner Field); Matthew Stockman/Allsport (Wrigley Field); Chris Trotman (Shea Stadium); Al Bello/Allsport (Keyspan Park); Elsa (Little League World Series).

THiS IS
BASEBALL COUNTRY

BASEBALL EVOLVED IN the mid-1800s from a less-developed game called "rounders." Originally played by grown men looking for some fun and a bit of exercise, it wasn't long before Americans of all ages caught on and the national pastime as we know it was born.

Today, baseball is as popular as ever. A lot has changed since those early years, but it's still very much the same game, creating a unique bond with the past for anyone who has picked up a bat or ball. From the blacktop pavement of New York City to the dusty cornfields of Nebraska to the sun-drenched diamonds of California, baseball still is the game of choice for millions of Americans — proving that this truly is "Baseball Country."

BASEBALL

WASHINGTON

MONTANA

MINNESOTA Twins

NORTH DAKOTA

OREGON

IDAHO

SOUTH DAKOTA

WYOMING

GIANTS

OAKLAND ATHLETICS A's

NEVADA

NEBRASK

UTAH

COLORADO ROCKIES

CALIFORNIA

COLORADO

KANSA

Dodgers

ARIZONA

NEW MEXICO

A

DIAMOND BACKS

TEXAS RANGERS T

SAN DIEGO Padres

TEX

4

Baltimore Orioles

Orioles shortstop **Cal Ripken** played in a record 2,632 consecutive games.

FIRST GAME: 1992

CAPACITY: 48,876

CITY TRIVIA

1. What local food are you most likely to find at Camden Yards?
A) Wiener schnitzel
B) Venison
C) Crab cakes

2. Whose record for consecutive games played did Cal Ripken break?
A) Lou Gehrig
B) Hank Aaron
C) Brooks Robinson

3. In what year was the United States' first railroad station built in Baltimore?
A) 1766
B) 1830
C) 1961

Answers on page 48

ABOUT ORIOLE PARK AT CAMDEN YARDS

Situated just minutes from Baltimore's beautiful Inner Harbor, Camden Yards is a wonderful destination — not just for Orioles fans, but for anyone who loves baseball. Located outside the stadium, just beyond the right-field wall on Eutaw St., is the famous B&O Warehouse, which at 1,016 feet is the longest building on the East Coast. In addition to the scenic surroundings, Camden Yards also is rich in history. Babe Ruth was born two blocks away and his father owned a tavern located in what is now shallow center field.

BALTIMORE

MARYLAND

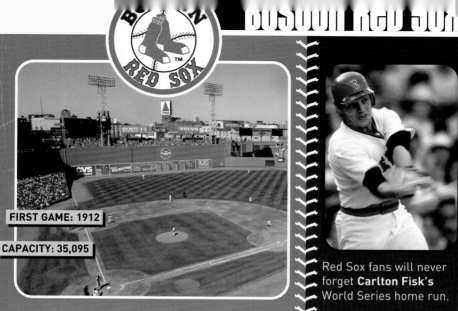

FIRST GAME: 1912

CAPACITY: 35,095

Red Sox fans will never forget **Carlton Fisk's** World Series home run.

ABOUT FENWAY PARK

The oldest stadium in the Majors is also one of the most unique. Fans can identify Boston's Fenway Park easily by its 37-foot-high wall in left field known as the "Green Monster." Many memorable games have been played at Fenway, including Game 6 of the 1975 World Series — considered by many to be the greatest game ever played — which Boston won on Carlton Fisk's 12th-inning home run that barely stayed fair. In 2004, the "Fenway faithful" (as Red Sox fans are sometimes called) celebrated their first world championship in 86 years.

BOSTON ▼

MASSACHUSETTS

CITY TRIVIA

4. What local college team did the Red Sox face in the first game at Fenway?
A) Harvard
B) Princeton
C) Duke

5. What Red Sox Hall of Famer is the last player to hit .400?
A) Carl Yastrzemski
B) Wade Boggs
C) Ted Williams

6. You can take the "T" to Fenway, which is fitting since the first _____ appeared in Boston in 1897.
A) trolley
B) taxi service
C) subway

Answers on page 48

The world champion **White Sox** had reason to celebrate last October.

FIRST GAME: 199
CAPACITY: 40,

CITY TRIVIA

7. Prior to being renamed in 2003, U.S. Cellular Field was known as what?
A) South Side Park
B) Comiskey Park
C) White Sox Field

8. Fans at U.S. Cellular can see _____, the tallest building in the U.S.
A) the White House
B) the Sears Tower
C) Wrigley Field

9. What division rival did Chicago beat in the first official game in AL history?
A) Cleveland
B) Kansas City
C) Detroit

Answers on page 48

8

ABOUT U.S. CELLULAR FIELD

When the White Sox opened the doors to their new stadium in 1991, they brought more than just memories of their former home with them. Fans loved the exploding scoreboard that would shoot of fireworks after a White Sox home run or victory at the old stadium, so one was installed in the new stadium. They even transported some of the dirt from the old infield onto the new one. In 2003, a record crowd of 47,609 was on hand for the All-Star Game. In 2005, the White Sox hosted their first World Series game since 1959 and won their first title since 1917.

CHICAGO

ILLINOIS

CLEVELAND INDIANS

FIRST GAME: 1994

CAPACITY: 43,405

Travis Hafner leads an up-and-coming Indians team with his mighty bat.

ABOUT JACOBS FIELD

Built in the heart of downtown, Jacobs Field has become one of Cleveland's most enjoyable attractions. A far cry from old Municipal Stadium, "The Jake" offers fans a cozy, comfortable place to watch a ballgame and keeps them entertained with its gigantic scoreboard, which includes the largest video screen in the Majors. Nestled within the boundaries of three bustling main streets in downtown Cleveland, Jacobs Field is so popular that, from 1995 to 2001, the Indians hosted a Major League-record 455 consecutive sell-outs. Just think of all the hot dogs they sold!

OHIO

CLEVELAND

CITY TRIVIA

10. What attraction has drawn more than 5,000,000 visitors since 1995?
A) Metroparks Zoo
B) Museum of Art
C) Rock and Roll Hall of Fame

11. Cleveland is the site of the only _____ in World Series history.
A) no-hitter
B) triple play
C) tie game

12. When is the last time the Indians won a world title?
A) 1948
B) 1995
C) Never

Answers on page 48

Detroit Tigers

Hall of Famer **Al Kaline,** known as "Mr. Tiger," spent 22 years in Detroit.

FIRST GAME: 2000

CAPACITY: 40,95

ABOUT COMERICA PARK

While the city of Detroit has been hard at work trying to restore many of its older neighborhoods with more modern buildings and attractions, the Tigers already have done their part by constructing gorgeous Comerica Park. Comerica honors past Tigers greats like Al Kaline and Ty Cobb with bronze statues beyond the outfield fence, while its modern features keep fans coming back for more. It also allows for great views of the city from most seats, and the carousel and Ferris wheel located within the park make it an attractive destination for even the youngest fans.

MICHIGAN

DETROIT

CITY TRIVIA

13. What famous record company started out in the "Motor City"?
A) Sony
B) Motown
C) Atlantic

14. Where did the Tigers play before Comerica was built?
A) Detroit Coliseum
B) Michigan Park
C) Tiger Stadium

15. What team's most recent World Series title was a 4-games-to-1 victory over Detroit in 1908?
A) The Cardinals
B) The Yankees
C) The Cubs

Answers on page 48

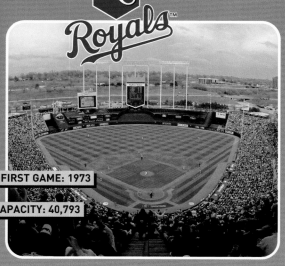

FIRST GAME: 1973

CAPACITY: 40,793

George Brett won the AL MVP Award in 1980 when he hit a whopping .390.

ABOUT KAUFFMAN STADIUM

Since opening its doors in 1973, Kauffman Stadium has provided millions of fans with an enjoyable atmosphere to watch a ballgame in. Until 1993, it was known as Royals Stadium, but was then renamed after Kansas City's original owner, Ewing Kauffman. The stadium's most distinctive feature is its 322-foot-wide "water spectacular" — the largest privately funded water fountain in the world. Many great moments have occurred at Kauffman Stadium, such as when the Royals celebrated the 1985 world title after storming back from 3-games-to-1 deficits in the ALCS and World Series.

KANSAS CITY

MISSOURI

CITY TRIVIA

16. What pro football team plays next door to Kauffman at Arrowhead Stadium?
A) The Chiefs
B) The Rams
C) The Colts

17. Who is the only Royal in the Baseball Hall of Fame?
A) Bo Jackson
B) Bret Saberhagen
C) George Brett

18. What Italian capital is the only city in the world with more fountains than K.C.'s 160?
A) Paris
B) Rome
C) London

Answers on page 48

Vladimir Guerrero has helped the Angels rise to the top of the AL West.

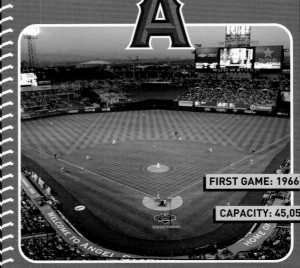

FIRST GAME: 1966

CAPACITY: 45,05

CITY TRIVIA

19. Not far from Hollywood, the first _____ opened in L.A. in 1902.
A) zoo
B) movie theater
C) theme park

20. What Angels player won an L.A. city championship in high school in 1989?
A) Vladimir Guerrero
B) Garret Anderson
C) Alex Rodriguez

21. What downtown L.A. stadium did the Angels call home in their first season?
A) Dodger Stadium
B) Anaheim Stadium
C) Wrigley Field

Answers on page 48

ABOUT ANGEL STADIUM

Although the ballpark has undergone numerous name changes and renovations (much like the team itself), the Angels have played at the same site since 1966. The ballpark was originally nicknamed "The Big A," after the giant, 230-foot-tall scoreboard that used to sit just beyond the outfield wall in left-center field. The Angels shared their home with the NFL's Los Angeles Rams for a number of years, during which time the seating capacity was increased to nearly 65,000. Angel Stadium is considerably smaller today, but with the Rally Monkey, ThunderStix and rabid fans present, it is no less noisy.

ANAHEIM

CALIFORNIA

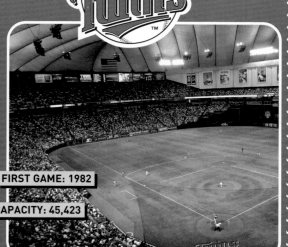

FIRST GAME: 1982

CAPACITY: 45,423

Kirby Puckett led the Twins to World Series victories in 1987 and '91.

ABOUT HUBERT H. HUMPHREY METRODOME

There's no denying that the Metrodome is one of the more unique Big League ballparks. First off, it's the only stadium where fans have to pass through revolving doors so that the air pressure inside stays high enough to keep the Teflon-coated fiberglass roof inflated. In fact, it takes 250,000 cubic feet of air pressure per minute to keep the roof from collapsing! Secondly, the Metrodome is the only stadium in the country that can boast that it has hosted four of the biggest events in the world of sports: the World Series, All-Star Game, Super Bowl and the NCAA men's Final Four.

MINNESOTA

MINNEAPOLIS ▼

CITY TRIVIA

22. The NBA's _____ played at the Metrodome during their first season.
A) Bulls
B) Lakers
C) Timberwolves

23. Minnesota went from last place to world champs in:
A) 1924
B) 1991
C) 2005

24. The Twins are named after the "Twin Cities" of:
A) Duluth and St. Cloud
B) Minneapolis and St. Paul
C) New York and L.A.

Answers on page 48

New York Yankees

FIRST GAME: 1923

CAPACITY: 57,478

The Yankees never won a World Series until **Babe Ruth** came to town.

ABOUT YANKEE STADIUM

In 1920, the Yankees did not have their own stadium yet, instead playing their home games at the Polo Grounds in Manhattan. With more fans coming out to see Babe Ruth and the Yankees than the Giants, the Polo Grounds' owners told the Yanks to find themselves a home of their own. Three years later, in 1923, "The House that Ruth Built" opened in the Bronx, with Ruth delivering a three-run homer in the inaugural game — a 4-1 win over the Red Sox. It was the first ballpark to be called a "stadium," and has seen the Yankees capture 39 American League pennants and 26 World Series titles since then.

NEW YORK

NEW YORK

FIRST GAME: 1968

CAPACITY: 43,662

Eric Chavez is one of Oakland's top hitters, driving in 101 runs in '05.

ABOUT McAFEE COLISEUM

The A's won three straight World Series titles in the mid-'70s at what was then known as Oakland Coliseum. Today, McAfee Coliseum looks much the same as it did back then. It is perhaps most recognizable as being one of the few stadiums where the bullpens are located within the field of play. Pitchers and catchers need to be alert while warming up, and if a batted ball remains on or under the bullpen bench, the hitter is awarded two bases. Although the first baseball game at the Coliseum took place in 1968, the first game was played back in 1966, when pro football's Raiders hosted the Chiefs.

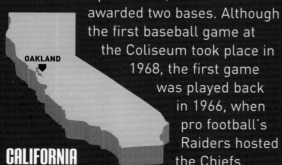

OAKLAND

CALIFORNIA

CITY TRIVIA

28. What caused a 10-day gap in the 1989 World Series between Oakland and San Francisco?
A) Earthquake
B) Forest fire
C) Umpires' strike

29. What *Forrest Gump* actor went to Oakland's Skyline High School?
A) Mel Gibson
B) Gary Sinise
C) Tom Hanks

30. What city has never been home to the A's franchise?
A) Kansas City
B) Philadelphia
C) Boston

Answers on page 48

Seattle Mariners

Ichiro Suzuki holds the single-season record for hits with 262 in 2004.

CITY TRIVIA

31. Where did the team play for its first 22 1/2 years?
A) Washington Park
B) The Kingdome
C) The Metrodome

32. The 605-foot-high _____ is Seattle's most well-known landmark.
A) Eiffel Tower
B) Space Needle
C) Mt. Rainier

33. Although the M's didn't arrive until 1977, what Major League team played in the city in 1969?
A) Seattle Pilots
B) Washington Mets
C) Olympus Titans

Answers on page 48

ABOUT SAFECO FIELD

The sweeping views of Puget Sound, the downtown Seattle skyline and Mt. Rainier combine with excellent sight lines from just about every seat in the house to make going to a game at Safeco Field an unforgettable experience. In order to provide the optimal playing surface, Safeco's turf actually is a blend of six different kinds of grasses. The retractable roof is designed to cover but not enclose the ballpark, and can be opened or closed in about 10 to 20 minutes with the push of a button. In 2001, when Seattle won an AL-record 116 games, more fans came to Safeco than any other field.

SEATTLE

WASHINGTON

FIRST GAME: 1998

CAPACITY: 43,772

Rocco Baldelli is one of several promising young Devil Rays players.

ABOUT TROPICANA FIELD

"The Trop" combines elements from baseball history with some Florida flavor at this distinctly modern complex. A 900-foot, tropical-themed, ceramic mosaic walkway — the largest in Florida — leads fans into the stadium via the rotunda, which was designed from the same blueprints used for a similar entrance at Ebbets Field (the former home of the Brooklyn Dodgers). On nights when the Devil Rays are off, the roof is illuminated orange to pay homage to the Tropicana juice company. It also is the first park in more than 20 years to feature artificial turf with all-dirt base paths.

FLORIDA

ST. PETERSBURG

CITY TRIVIA

34. What manager led the D-Rays to a franchise-record 70 wins in 2004?
A) Jack McKeon
B) Hal McRae
C) Lou Piniella

35. What was "The Trop" called when the NHL's Lightning played there?
A) Storm Center
B) ThunderDome
C) The Bolthouse

36. The Devil Rays' Spring Training home is _____ miles from Tropicana?
A) less than two
B) more than 100
C) nearly 1,000

Answers on page 48

Texas Rangers

Nolan Ryan ended his 27-year career in a Rangers uniform.

FIRST GAME: 1994

CAPACITY: 49,115

CITY TRIVIA

37. Texas is the _____ state in the continental U.S.
A) smallest
B) largest
C) rainiest

38. Nolan Ryan threw the seventh and final _____ of his career in 1991.
A) shutout
B) wild pitch
C) no-hitter

39. Prior to 1972, the Rangers played in the nation's capital and were called the:
A) D.C. United
B) Capital Gamers
C) Washington Senators

Answers on page 48

ABOUT AMERIQUEST FIELD

Everything about the Rangers' home stadium has a Texas feel to it. The architects used many of the design elements native to the area, "Lone Stars" can be found throughout the stadium, and the Nolan Ryan Expressway serves as a major access road through the complex. Additionally, the proximity of the fans to the action on the field is among the closest in the Major Leagues. Behind the right-field home run porch lies the Legends of the Game Baseball Museum, complete with a 225-seat auditorium and theater. In order to combat the strong Texas winds, the playing field sits 22 feet below street level.

ARLINGTON

TEXAS

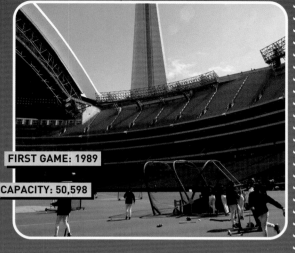

FIRST GAME: 1989

CAPACITY: 50,598

Joe Carter will always hold a special place in the hearts of Blue Jays fans.

ABOUT ROGERS CENTRE

Toronto's Rogers Centre truly is one of the most unique stadiums in the world. The only Major League stadium left outside America, it houses four restaurants, a hotel and the world's largest Jumbotron scoreboard. Its majestic retractable roof — the first stadium to feature one — also makes it the tallest park in the Bigs. The pitcher's mound is constructed on a fiberglass dish and can be lowered or raised by a hydraulic system, and the field can be converted into use as a football stadium for the CFL's Toronto Argonauts in fewer than 12 hours.

ONTARIO

TORONTO

CITY TRIVIA

40. Toronto's _____, at 1,815 feet, is the tallest building in the world.
A) CN Tower
B) Sears Tower
C) Space Needle

41. What former Blue Jay hit a walk-off homer to end the 1993 Fall Classic?
A) Joe Carter
B) John Olerud
C) Paul Molitor

42. The world record for inflated _____ in an enclosed area (46) was set here.
A) blimps
B) hot air balloons
C) parade floats

Answers on page 48

Arizona Diamondbacks

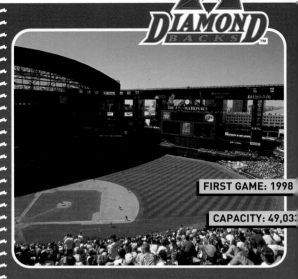

FIRST GAME: 1998

CAPACITY: 49,03:

Luis Gonzalez led the D'Backs to a world title in the team's fourth year.

CITY TRIVIA

43. What famous natural landmark is located in Arizona?
A) Mount Rushmore
B) Niagara Falls
C) Grand Canyon

44. Which Arizona player's bloop single won the 2001 World Series?
A) Luis Gonzalez
B) Mariano Rivera
C) Craig Counsell

45. Which one of these events has Chase NOT hosted?
A) Women's college basketball
B) Rose Bowl
C) Arizona National Boat Show

Answers on page 48

ABOUT CHASE FIELD

When fans visit Chase Field, they get to experience much more than just a baseball game. From its signature swimming pool beyond the right-center-field wall to its retractable roof, the home of the Diamondbacks is filled with modern-day nooks and crannies. Sitting 1,100 feet above sea level — the second-highest park in the Majors — Chase offers fans nearly a quarter mile of concession stands, an air-conditioned venue in which to watch games and, on a per-game basis, a chance to rent and take a dip in the MasterCard Pool Pavilion, the only on-site swimming pool in the Majors.

PHOENIX

ARIZONA

Braves

FIRST GAME: 1997

CAPACITY: 50,096

ABOUT TURNER FIELD

Even before Turner Field became home to the Braves, it housed plenty of competitive action as the site of the 1996 Summer Olympic Games. The park's most unique feature is the Grand Entry Plaza. The Plaza is a food and entertainment venue that appeals to children with Tooner Field — a cartoon-themed inter-active area where kids can challenge their baseball skills — and adults, with Monument Grove, which pays tribute to all-time Braves greats. Adults and children alike can enjoy the Ivan Allen Jr. Braves Museum & Hall of Fame that traces the Braves' history.

♥ATLANTA

GEORGIA

Hall of Famer **Hank Aaron** hit a remarkable 755 homers in his career.

CITY TRIVIA

46. Which famous media mogul is the Braves' stadium named after?
A) Tina Turner
B) Ted Turner
C) Rupert Murdoch

47. Which former Brave is the all-time home run leader?
A) Eddie Mathews
B) Willie Mays
C) Hank Aaron

48. Turner Field was inspired by which early-'90s American League ballpark?
A) Oriole Park at Camden Yards
B) Coors Field
C) Comerica Park

Answers on page 48

A healthy **Mark Prior** could be the Cubs' key to a World Series trip.

FIRST GAME: 1914

CAPACITY: 39,53

ABOUT WRIGLEY FIELD

While the most notable feature about Wrigley Field may be the ivy covering the outfield walls, the charm of this ballpark extends much further. Built on the grounds once occupied by a school that was used for religious teachings, it is the second-oldest ballpark in the Majors, two years younger than Boston's Fenway Park. For its first 74 years, all games at Wrigley were played during the day, but that changed when lights were added in 1988. The first official night game occurred on Aug. 9, 1988, when the Cubs defeated the Mets, 6-4.

CHICAGO

ILLINOIS

FIRST GAME: 2003

CAPACITY: 42,059

Among many career high-lights for **Joe Morgan** are two titles with the Reds.

ABOUT GREAT AMERICAN BALL PARK

As Major League Baseball's first officially recognized franchise, the Reds made sure that their home represented this rich history. Great American Ball Park pays tribute to the team's past with statues, mosaics, banners recognizing famous dates and a nostalgic Sun/Moon Deck. The 1869 team mosaic that greets fans as they enter the park probably is the most striking connection with the past. The retired numbers of Johnny Bench, Joe Morgan and Frank Robinson, among others, are prominently featured in the ballpark, as well.

OHIO

CINCINNATI

CITY TRIVIA

52. What other city in Ohio is home to a Major League Baseball team?
A) Akron
B) Cleveland
C) Milwaukee

53. What river is Great American Ball Park located near?
A) Ohio River
B) Mississippi River
C) Delaware River

54. What was the nickname of the Reds' 1976 world championship team?
A) Murderer's Row
B) Big Red Machine
C) Harvey's Wallbangers

Answers on page 48

COLORADO ROCKIES

FIRST GAME: 1995

CAPACITY: 50,449

Clint Barmes is a huge part of the Rockies' plan to return to the playoffs.

CITY TRIVIA

55. In which Colorado city do the Rockies play?
A) Boulder
B) Salt Lake City
C) Denver

56. Which Colorado team did the Rockies share a home with for their first two seasons?
A) Colorado Avalanche
B) Denver Broncos
C) Denver Nuggets

57. Which pitcher threw the only no-hitter at Coors Field?
A) Hideo Nomo
B) Jason Jennings
C) Randy Johnson

Answers on page 48

ABOUT COORS FIELD

The thin air of Coors Field has made the Rockies' home a thrill for hitters and a nightmare for pitchers. The field sits nearly one mile above sea level, with the 20th row of the upper deck painted purple to indicate the exact one-mile plateau, making it the highest park in the Majors. Since it hosted its first game in 1995, Coors Field has become the most hitter-friendly park ever built, owning the record for the most homers hit in a stadium in one season with 303 in 1999. Before moving to Coors Field, the Rockies played their first two seasons at Mile High Stadium. Coors has increased its seating capacity three times to accomodate the area's large number of fans.

COLORADO

DENVER

FIRST GAME: 1993

CAPACITY: 36,331

In 2003, **Dontrelle Willis** won NL Rookie of the Year honors and a world title.

ABOUT DOLPHINS STADIUM

When it comes to their home turf, the Marlins have a roommate of sorts, sharing their ballpark with the NFL's Miami Dolphins, after whom the stadium is named. The first baseball game ever to take place at the park was an exhibition contest between the Baltimore Orioles and Los Angeles Dodgers in 1988 — five years before the Marlins even came into existence. Since it was not originally built to house a baseball team, Dolphins Stadium can be a tricky playing field. It also has its own version of Fenway Park's "Green Monster" in left field, a 26 1/2-foot wall known as the "Teal Monster."

FLORIDA

MIAMI

CITY TRIVIA

58. What is Florida's most famous attraction?
A) Disneyland
B) Disney World
C) EuroDisney

59. Who did the Marlins beat to win their first World Series in 1997?
A) The Yankees
B) The Indians
C) The Braves

60. Florida has won two world titles in its history. How many World Series have the Marlins lost?
A) Five
B) Three
C) None

Answers on page 48

After 18 years in Houston, **Craig Biggio** finally played in the Fall Classic in 2005.

FIRST GAME: 2000

CAPACITY: 40,950

CITY TRIVIA

61. The Astros won their first _____ in 2005.
A) World Series
B) National League pennant
C) playoff game

62. Who were the original "Killer B's"?
A) Biggio & Berkman
B) Bagwell & Burke
C) Bagwell & Biggio

63. Minute Maid Park is connected to the nearly century-old Union Station. What is Union Station?
A) A bus depot
B) A railroad station
C) A subway station

Answers on page 48

ABOUT MINUTE MAID PARK

When Minute Maid Park opened in 2000, it brought open-air baseball back to Houston for the first time in 36 years, thanks to the 242-foot high retractable roof. People were excited about this, as more than 3 million fans visited Minute Maid that year. Some distinctive features of the park include the Crawford Boxes, which are 763 seats that jut out over the left-field wall; Tal's Hill — a 10-degree angled hill in center field; and a full-size replica of a 19th-century Wild West steam locomotive that runs on a track located above left field. In 2005, Minute Maid Park hosted the first World Series ever played in Texas.

HOUSTON

TEXAS

FIRST GAME: 1962

CAPACITY: 56,000

Sandy Koufax set the standard for southpaws during his 12-year career.

ABOUT DODGER STADIUM

Since opening in 1962, Dodger Stadium has hosted its share of events, from Olympic baseball in 1984 to a mass by Pope John Paul II in 1987 to entertainers such as the Rolling Stones and The Beatles to, of course, some of the best baseball ever played. Among the highlights is Game 1 of the 1988 World Series, better known as the "Kirk Gibson Game." In the ninth inning of that contest, Gibson, with two bad legs, hobbled to the plate as a pinch-hitter and launched a 3-2 pitch over the fence for a game-winning two-run homer. As Dodger Stadium broke out in pandemonium, Gibson limped his way around the bases.

LOS ANGELES

CALIFORNIA

CITY TRIVIA

64. What East Coast site was home to the Dodgers prior to 1958?
A) Brooklyn
B) Philadelphia
C) Baltimore

65. What nickname does Dodger Stadium also go by, due to its exact location?
A) L.A. Stadium
B) Chavez Ravine
C) California Field

66. Which AL team also played here from 1962 to 1965?
A) The Angels
B) The Blue Jays
C) The Tigers

Answers on page 48

MILWAUKEE BREWERS

In 1999, **Robin Yount** became the first Brewers player in the Hall of Fame.

FIRST GAME: 2001

CAPACITY: 41,900

CITY TRIVIA

67. Who was the Brewers' owner from 1970 to '98?
A) Commissioner Bud Selig
B) Manager Ned Yost
C) Robin Yount

68. More than 35 percent of the nation's _____ is made in Wisconsin.
A) yogurt
B) cheese
C) flour

69. What NL team called Milwaukee its home before the Brewers arrived?
A) The Braves
B) The Yankees
C) The Dodgers

Answers on page 48

ABOUT MILLER PARK

Miller Park boasts something that no other building in North America can — the only fan-shaped convertible roof. This 12,000-ton, seven-panel roof, which opens and closes almost silently in just 10 minutes, guarantees perfect playing conditions for the Brewers. Inside the stadium, the roof reaches 200 feet above the playing field, while outside, the highest arch towers 30 stories high, making it a fixture in Milwaukee's skyline. The park is located in what used to be the center-field parking lot of the Brewers' former home from 1970 to 2000, County Stadium.

MILWAUKEE

WISCONSIN

28

FIRST GAME: 1964

CAPACITY: 57,369

Pedro Martinez took his game to New York in 2005 and continued to impress.

ABOUT SHEA STADIUM

Shea Stadium has been the sight of many great performances in both baseball and pop culture history. It was at this Flushing, Queens, location that more than 55,000 fans assembled for The Beatles' first major outdoor concert in the United States on Aug. 15, 1965. It also was here where the infamous "It gets by Buckner!" game took place — Game 6 of the 1986 World Series — eventually leading to a Game 7 that the Mets won. Shea Stadium is adjacent to the location of the 1964-65 World's Fair and also is next door to Arthur Ashe Stadium, where the annual tennis tournament, the U.S. Open, takes place.

NEW YORK

NEW YORK

CITY TRIVIA

70. Shea is less than 10 miles away from what other Big League park?
A) Yankee Stadium
B) Camden Yards
C) Turner Field

71. What pops out of a hat at Shea whenever a Met homers?
A) A rabbit
B) A big apple
C) A banana

72. What stadium did the Mets use as their home park before Shea was completed?
A) Polo Grounds
B) Yankee Stadium
C) Fenway Park

Answers on page 48

PHILADELPHIA PHILLIES

Mike Schmidt did it all in Philly, becoming one of the game's best players.

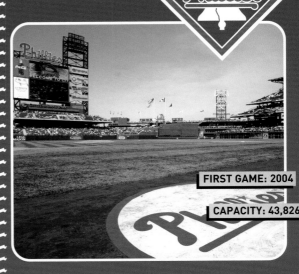

FIRST GAME: 2004

CAPACITY: 43,826

CITY TRIVIA

73. Who did the Phillies play in the 1993 World Series?
A) The Twins
B) The Blue Jays
C) The Yankees

74. Where did the Phillies play before Citizens Bank Park?
A) Veterans Stadium
B) Candlestick Park
C) Shea Stadium

75. What famous event in U.S. history took place in Philly?
A) Battle of Gettysburg
B) Signing of the Declaration of Independence
C) Boston Tea Party

Answers on page 48

ABOUT CITIZENS BANK PARK

A day at Citizens Bank Park offers fans a crash course in local cuisine. While the traditional peanuts and Cracker Jack are available, the menu is highlighted by cheesesteaks, Philly-style sandwiches, gourmet pizza, the famous Philadelphia sandwich "The Schmitter," crab fries and Turkey Hill ice cream. To further the Philadelphia experience, a giant replica of the Liberty Bell towers 100 feet above street level in right-center field and rings whenever the Phillies launch a homer. Ashburn's Alley — a festive outfield entertainment area that is open to all visitors — is named after Phillies legend Richie Ashburn.

PHILADELPHIA

PENNSYLVANIA

FIRST GAME: 2001

CAPACITY: 38,127

84 LUMBER

The Pirates hope young players like **Jason Bay** can turn the club around.

ABOUT PNC PARK

Sitting on the north shore of the Allegheny River, PNC Park is a classic-style ballpark that combines aspects of modern-day Pittsburgh with the spirit of early parks such as Forbes Field, Wrigley Field and Fenway Park. Its rhythmic arch-ways and steel trusswork provide PNC with an old-time feel, while its 69 suites, out-door river terrace and riverwalk give fans ultimate comfort. Adding to the experience is an ideal sight line, with the highest seat only 88 feet from the field, thanks to PNC Park's two-deck design — the first park to be built with just two decks since 1953.

Pittsburgh has been home to the Pirates for more than 110 years.

PITTSBURGH

PENNSYLVANIA

CITY TRIVIA

76. The right-field wall rises 21 feet to honor _____, who wore No. 21.
A) Roberto Clemente
B) Willie Stargell
C) Babe Ruth

77. The 1979 world champion Pirates adopted _____ as their theme song.
A) "I Will Survive"
B) "Hollaback Girl"
C) "We Are Family"

78. What Pittsburgh native and current Pirate got the first hit at PNC Park?
A) Barry Bonds
B) Jason Bay
C) Sean Casey

Answers on page 48

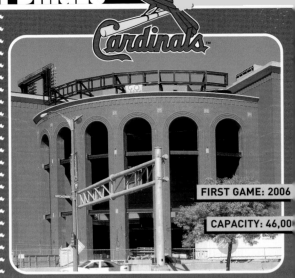

FIRST GAME: 2006

CAPACITY: 46,00

Albert Pujols won his first of what could be many MVP Awards in 2005.

CITY TRIVIA

79. What St. Louis landmark is visible from most seats at the new stadium?
A) Mississippi River
B) Gateway Arch
C) White House

80. What event has been played in St. Louis each of the past two years?
A) All-Star Game
B) NLCS
C) World Series

81. Part of Busch Stadium's design is based on what St. Louis bridge?
A) Eads Bridge
B) Brooklyn Bridge
C) London Bridge

Answers on page 48

ABOUT BUSCH STADIUM

After 40 years at the old Busch Stadium, the Cardinals moved into their new home in 2006. The new stadium has some things in common with the old, including the same name and practically the same location — just next door to the Cardinals' former home. But it wasn't easy getting ready for Opening Day. Since the new stadium was built on land occupied by the old one, construction could not be completed until the 2005 season ended, leading the project to stretch into the spring of '06. Unlike the enclosed bowl of old Busch, the new park allows open views of the city's famous sights and downtown buildings.

ST. LOUIS

MISSOURI

![Padres]

FIRST GAME: 2004

CAPACITY: 42,500

Tony Gwynn hit over .300 for 19 straight years and won eight batting titles.

ABOUT PETCO PARK

Fans don't even need a seat to enjoy a game at Petco Park. Not only does the ballpark feature breathtaking views of San Diego, but it also provides fans with standing-room areas distributed throughout the stadium and lawn seating opportunities in an elevated grass park located directly behind the outfield wall dubbed the "Park at the Park." One of Petco's most recognizable features is the 95-year-old Western Metal Supply Company building, which sits in left field and was incorporated into the park's design, rather than being torn down. Also on site are the Padres Hall of Fame and a 250-seat auditorium.

SAN DIEGO

CALIFORNIA

CITY TRIVIA

82. What is Petco Park's most unique concession item?
A) Fish tacos
B) Peanuts
C) Dodger Dogs

83. What country's border with the U.S. is less than a half hour drive from San Diego?
A) Canada
B) Japan
C) Mexico

84. On what street, named for a Padres legend, is Petco Park located?
A) Tony Gwynn Dr.
B) Bruce Bochy Way
C) Jake Peavy Terr.

Answers on page 48

Willie Mays is one of the best all-around players ever to put on a uniform.

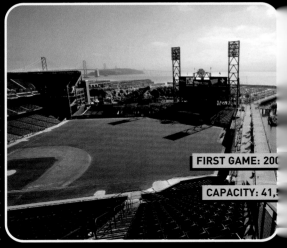

FIRST GAME: 200

CAPACITY: 41,

CITY TRIVIA

85. What Giants player has hit the most home runs into McCovey Cove?
A) Willie Mays
B) Barry Bonds
C) Jason Schmidt

86. Until they moved out west in 1958, the Giants played at what stadium?
A) Polo Grounds
B) Shea Stadium
C) Yankee Stadium

87. What rival visited San Francisco for the first game at the new park?
A) The Cubs
B) The Yankees
C) The Dodgers

Answers on page 48

ABOUT SBC PARK

Fans at a Giants game experience much more than just the play on the field. The ballpark provides sweeping views of the San Francisco Bay, glimpses of Berkeley and Oakland in the distance, and those in the right-field upper deck can catch a view of the Bay Bridge. Inspired by the likes of Wrigley Field and Fenway Park, the home of the Giants was modeled after Camden Yards, Jacobs Field and Coors Field. Fans who enter the stadium by the public entrance are greeted by a statue of Willie Mays, while monstrous home runs to right field splash into part of the bay dubbed McCovey Cove after Willie McCovey.

SAN FRANCISCO

CALIFORNIA

NATIONALS

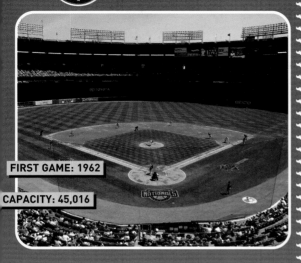

FIRST GAME: 1962

CAPACITY: 45,016

Livan Hernandez is among the most durable starters in the game.

ABOUT RFK STADIUM

Originally named D.C. Stadium, this ballpark took its current name of Robert F. Kennedy Memorial Stadium in 1969 in memory of the late U.S. Senator. Politics always has been intertwined with baseball in D.C., with U.S. presidents traditionally opening each new season by throwing out the first pitch. President George W. Bush renewed that tradition on April 14, 2005, when baseball returned to the nation's capital after a 34-year hiatus. When the stadium first opened in 1961, it housed both professional football and baseball. Today, Major League Soccer's D.C. United also uses the stadium.

RFK STADIUM

WASHINGTON, D.C.

CITY TRIVIA

88. Washington is just 38 miles from which AL city?
A) Seattle
B) Baltimore
C) Kansas City

89. Prior to Bush, who was the last President to throw out the first pitch?
A) Abraham Lincoln
B) Bill Clinton
C) Richard Nixon

90. Which current Big League team was the last to play in D.C. before the Nationals?
A) The Giants
B) The Rangers
C) The Twins

Answers on page 48

events

NO ONE COULD have predicted that in back-to-back seasons, the Red Sox would end their 86-year World Series drought and the White Sox would win their first world title in 88 years. As the 2006 season unfolds, fans throughout the country, and around the world, surely will keep an eye on all the action to see which team will surprise us next.

It all begins on Sunday, April 2, when the defending champion White Sox kick off the season by hosting the division rival Cleveland Indians. In July, the baseball world will turn its focus toward Pittsburgh, when PNC Park hosts the 77th All-Star Game on July 11. The National League will be seeking its first victory in the Midsummer Classic since 1996.

Not long after the All-Star Game ends does the real excitement begin. As the season winds down, the pennant races heat up, with some teams battling it out until the final weekend for a trip to the postseason. For the eight teams fortunate enough to move on, baseball's playoffs are the ultimate survival test. Every game is played in front of a packed stadium, with millions more watching at home to see who will be the next World Series champion.

Minor Leagues

KEYSPAN PARK IN CONEY ISLAND, N.Y.

MINOR LEAGUE BASEBALL has long been referred to as the "Bush Leagues" — a slang term that implies that Minor League ball is not necessarily ready for wide exposure and competition. Well, based on attendance at these games, that doesn't seem to be true.

More than 35 million fans have attended Minor League games in each of the past seven seasons. Minor League Baseball, which consists of four different levels of competition (rookie ball, Single-A, Double-A and Triple-A), is where players develop their skills before the best ones graduate to the Majors. More than 300 teams play in cities across the U.S. from Rochester, N.Y., to Spokane, Wash. North Carolina alone is host to 11 Minor League clubs, including the Tampa Bay Devil Rays-affiliated Durham Bulls — the inspiration for the classic film, *Bull Durham*.

Minor League games allow fans to see players — many of whom go on to become Big League stars — up close and personal.

Spring Training

THERE ARE FEW experiences like stepping foot into a baseball palace for the first time. Think Wrigley Field, Yankee Stadium, Fenway Park — the truly regal ballparks that dot the American landscape.

But on a smaller scale, the parks that house Big League teams for the months of February and March offer an experience that can be equally enjoyable. Instead of the immense Dodger Stadium, fans can watch the Los Angeles ballclub work out at Holman Stadium in Vero Beach, Fla., where players and coaches have biked around the "Dodgertown" grounds since 1948. Or they can watch the A's from the Phoenix Municipal Stadium stands, where views of desert mountains and cacti replace the towering rows of seats that fill up Oakland's enormous McAfee Coliseum.

LEGENDS FIELD IN TAMPA, FLA.

All 30 teams trek to either Arizona or Florida for six weeks of Spring Training. There, fans can watch Big Leaguers run drills and practice just like Little Leaguers do. And you can even see your favorite players take part in exhibition games from seats much closer than you probably could get for a regular-season game. The coolest part (aside from the perfect weather, of course) is seeing players running laps along the outfield wall after they've been subbed out, even while the game is still going on. You can be sure you won't see that during the regular season!

ARIZONA'S TEMPE DIABLO STADIUM

There are nine Spring Training stadiums in Arizona, and seven of them are within about a 45-minute drive of downtown Phoenix. The other two stadiums (one of which is shared by the Diamondbacks and White Sox) are in Tucson. Some of the stadiums are so close to one another that you can easily check out a day game at one and a night game at another. Be sure to visit Scottsdale Stadium, where the Giants train, and Surprise Stadium, the newest site in Arizona, which is home to the Rangers and Royals.

In sunny Florida, there are 17 stadium sites, with the Cardinals and Marlins sharing Roger Dean Stadium in Jupiter. The stadiums are more spread out here than in the Arizona locations, but a good number are concentrated in three areas — there are seven parks within an hour's drive from Tampa, four others within about 90 minutes of Palm Beach and five more that are within an hour of Orlando. Legends Field in Tampa, spring home of the Yankees, is not to be missed. The field dimensions are exactly the same as those at Yankee Stadium, so you can get a pretty good idea about how well the team will perform when it moves north.

SHRINES

You can definitely get your fill of baseball by attending a Big League game. But if you want something a little different, there are some other great options around the country.

In Cooperstown, N.Y., a tiny village that bleeds history, the National Baseball Hall of Fame and Museum is a must-see attraction. Walk around the exhibits, looking at pieces of the game's past, making sure to view the plaques for each Hall of Famer. And if you head over to Doubleday Field, there's a chance that you could even see a game going on. Every year, two Big League teams play each other in the Hall of Fame Game, the only exhibition game that takes place during the season.

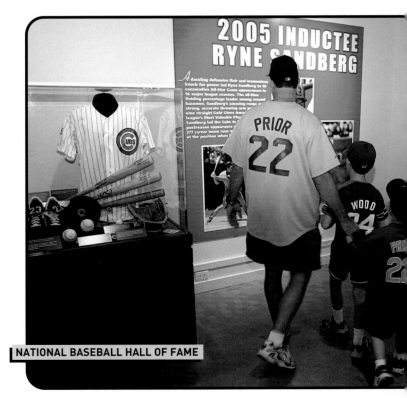

NATIONAL BASEBALL HALL OF FAME

LITTLE LEAGUE WORLD SERIES

If you'd prefer to see people *making* history rather than just reading about it, be sure to check out the nation's top amateur events. Every June, the best college baseball teams in the country meet to determine the NCAA champion at the College World Series in Omaha, Neb., while the nation's top college softball teams fight for the

NCAA title at the Women's College World Series in Oklahoma City. Nowhere else in sports can you find the pageantry of these two events, with the fans and players truly taking over the two cities.

Finally, the Little League World Series in Williamsport, Pa., is an event that everyone should attend at least once in their lives. With the best 11- and 12-year-old baseball players in the world squaring off, the games are great. But there's nothing like seeing the kids just being kids, hanging out in the pool together, trading pins and communicating with each other despite not speaking the same language. Tickets are always free, so there's no reason not to go! If you're on the West Coast and can't make it to Williamsport, consider a trip to Portland, Ore., in August for the Little League Softball World Series.

Baseball Country
WORLDWIDE

CALLING BASEBALL "AMERICA'S pastime" may not be totally accurate anymore.

While the game certainly has flourished in the United States for more than a century now, it also has become very popular all around the world. In fact, more than 100 National Baseball Federations exist worldwide, fueling the emergence of players from countries such as Argentina, Australia, Brazil, China, Germany, Italy, Korea, the Netherlands, New Zealand and South Africa, on top of already-established baseball hotbeds like Japan, Puerto Rico and the Dominican Republic.

To celebrate this growth of baseball, the first ever World Baseball Classic will be played in March 2006. The 16-team, four-round tournament will crown the most dominant baseball nation. It will feature Major and Minor League stars, as well as professional and amateur players from around the world, who will play for their native lands.

HIRAM BITHORN STADIUM

The World Baseball Classic is partly the result of Major League Baseball's efforts to expand the game around the globe. Initiatives like the Australian and European academies and the Envoy Program send top coaches and players to all different countries to help those places develop an interest in baseball and to assist players from those countries in improving their skills.

ICHIRO SUZUKI

The tradition of Major League games being played outside of the 50 states — such as Opening Day in Japan in 2000 and 2004 — was taken to a new level in 2003 and '04 when the Expos (now the Nationals) made Puerto Rico their temporary home by playing 22 games at San Juan's Hiram Bithorn Stadium in each of those two seasons.

If the excitement in Puerto Rico didn't convince people of baseball's popularity around the world, then the World Baseball Classic and the Major League rosters that are filled with foreign-born players should do the trick.

City Tracker

Date	City	Stadium	Visiting Team

NOW THAT YOU'VE learned all about Baseball Country, it's time to hit the road. Every time you go to a baseball game, enter the information into this chart. That way, you'll remember everything about it, like who pitched, who hit home runs and who won.

How quickly can you fill it up?

SCORE	WINNING PITCHER	HOME RUNS	WHO DID I GO WITH?

FUN & GAMES

Word Find

More often than not, Major League teams play in large cities with lots of fans. The Twins, for example, play in Minneapolis — Minnesota's largest city. Hidden below are 15 teams that play in the most populated cities in their states. How many can you find? Team names are listed in all directions: forward, backward, up, down and diagonally.

ASTROS

BRAVES

BREWERS

DIAMONDBACKS

DODGERS

MARINERS

ORIOLES

PHILLIES

RED SOX

ROCKIES

ROYALS

TIGERS

TWINS

WHITE SOX

YANKEES

```
F X B K E A M L E T S U K P C R
J C O P C H B R A V E S O E M D
Q M L S B R B V S P O I P J S A
T X C S E A D H Q R D T Y R N R
R B J W K T G U T S G I E X Q V
N S E T S C I S F P F G H W M E
I R M A R L A H K L D E J T R S
S L A Y O R E B W O T R Z E A O
E E R X S C U E D W E S D S P S
L S I E S S F V T N F S R E R N
O G N Z C E S Q S V O U J I I B
I F E A D E N B G X R M T L B F
R E R O C K I E S D C L A L S S
O D S V W N W D Z H K M Q I T N
S T O E W A T B Y N J X U H D G
H F L M G Y E N K O N J D P I C
```

Name That Stadium

1. Known for its ivy-covered outfield wall
2. Located near Baltimore's Inner Harbor
3. Nicknamed "The House That Ruth Built"
4. Located on the shores of the Allegheny River
5. Oldest Major League ballpark

A. Yankee Stadium
B. Fenway Park
C. PNC Park
D. Camden Yards
E. Wrigley Field

What State Am I From?

From Alaska to Florida, Major Leaguers come from just about every state in the country. You never know — some of them might have grown up near your hometown! The players named below come from all different places. Read the clues they've given you and try to figure out which state each player grew up in.

1. **Lance Berkman, Houston Astros, three-time All-Star**
   - In 1976, I was born in a town called Waco and I later attended Canyon High School in New Braunfels.
   - I stayed in my home state for college by attending Rice University, where I drove in 134 runs in 63 games in 1997.
   - I was taken by one of two professional teams in my home state in the first round of the 1997 draft.
   - My home state is the largest in size of the lower 48 states.

2. **Chad Cordero, Washington Nationals, MLB saves leader in 2005**
   - Since becoming a Big Leaguer, I've donated equipment to my old baseball team at Don Lugo High School.
   - I pitched in the College World Series twice — in 2001 and 2003 — with a school from my home state.
   - My first appearance as a Major Leaguer in my home state came on April 27, 2004, against the Padres.
   - My home state has the highest population of any state in the country.

3. **Chris Carpenter, St. Louis Cardinals, 2005 NL Cy Young Award winner**
   - I grew up in a town called Raymond, where I played Little League Baseball.
   - I went to Trinity High School in Manchester, where we were good enough to have won a state title in 1992.
   - I still live in my home state, where our motto is "Live Free or Die."
   - My home state is located within New England and is so far north that it actually borders Canada.

4. **Ryan Howard, Philadelphia Phillies, 2005 NL Rookie of the Year**
   - The closest Big League ballpark to my hometown is Busch Stadium.
   - In my first varsity baseball game for Lafayette High School, I hit two home runs and had seven RBI.
   - I went to the same in-state college as fellow "Show Me Stater" Bill Mueller.
   - My home state is surrounded by eight other states and is bordered by the Mississippi River on the east.

ANSWER KEY

City Trivia

After you've completed every team's "City Trivia" section, match up your answers with the ones given here to see how many you got right. A lot of them were pretty tricky, so don't be upset if you got some wrong! The scoring system works as follows:

1-30 correct: **Triple-A** – Congratulations! You're almost ready for the Big Leagues.

31-60 correct: **Major Leagues** – Good job! Your knowledge of baseball makes you a real pro.

61-90 correct: **All-Star** – Wow! You deserve a plaque in the Hall of Fame.

1-C; 2-A; 3-B; 4-A; 5-C; 6-C; 7-B; 8-B; 9-A; 10-C; 11-B; 12-A; 13-B; 14-C; 15-C; 16-A; 17-C; 18-B; 19-B; 20-B; 21-C; 22-C; 23-B; 24-B; 25-C; 26-A; 27-B; 28-A; 29-C; 30-C; 31-B; 32-B; 33-A; 34-C; 35-B; 36-A; 37-B; 38-C; 39-C; 40-A; 41-A; 42-B; 43-C; 44-A; 45-B; 46-B; 47-C; 48-A; 49-B; 50-B; 51-C; 52-B; 53-A; 54-B; 55-C; 56-B; 57-A; 58-B; 59-B; 60-C; 61-B; 62-C; 63-B; 64-A; 65-B; 66-A; 67-A; 68-B; 69-A; 70-A; 71-B; 72-A; 73-B; 74-A; 75-B; 76-A; 77-C; 78-C; 79-B; 80-B; 81-A; 82-A; 83-C; 84-A; 85-B; 86-A; 87-C; 88-B; 89-C; 90-B

Fun & Games

Word Find

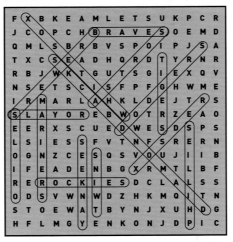

What State Am I From?

Berkman – Texas; Cordero – California; Carpenter – New Hampshire; Howard – Missouri

Name That Stadium

1-E; 2-D; 3-A; 4-C; 5-B

48